ROBERT
FROST
COUNTRY

Betsy and Tom Melvin

ROBERT
FROST
COUNTRY

Foreword by William Meredith

A Dolphin Book

Doubleday & Company, Inc.   Garden City, New York   1978

We dedicate this work to our mothers, Ethel Stewart Blake
and Gerta Pollak Slunsky, who, in separate worlds,
taught us the value of industry, aesthetics, and perseverance.

ACKNOWLEDGMENTS

Our humble thanks go to Ted Sirlin, currently president of the Professional Photographers' Association of America, who, six years ago, first suggested the idea of this book.

John Doscher taught Betsy "not to be a location hunter, but to see what you have where you are." He was the first to impress her with the skillful utilization of light. Adolph Fassbender taught her to find the beauty inherent in any subject; his disciplines' and concepts have served us well.

Our local Essex Center third- and fourth-graders, by their spontaneous acclaim, convinced us that Frost's poetry had, indeed, sprung to life for them through our photographs!

Through the Professional Photographers' Associations of Vermont, New England and America, and our regional school, the New England Institute of Professional Photography, we avail ourselves of every opportunity to learn and achieve new levels of competence in our profession.

We thank the dedicated technicians, especially at Meisel Photochrome and Photographers' Color Service, who assure us of top-quality photographs.

We wish gratefully to acknowledge the help of Robert Frost's great friend, Alfred C. Edwards. And our special thanks to our agents Paul Reynolds and John Sterling; and to our editor, Patrick Filley.

Thanks go to our many inspired friends who encouraged us to publish this work for the benefit of all who love Robert Frost's poetry and the beauty of Nature's realm.

PHOTOGRAPHERS' NOTES

When I first came upon the lines that have become so familiar to me, I realized that Robert Frost had said in his beautiful poetry what I had felt in my heart when I made many of the photographs, through my medium of creative expression. It is significant that only three of all these pictures were made especially for this volume.

All of these photographs were made in the past ten years, many of them under my former name, Betsy Thrasher, before The Artistic Alliance came into being. In these past five years, since we are both working creative photographers, it has been important to me to feature our joint name. During this time, Tom and I have made a group of these photographs together, hardly knowing who had actually taken any particular picture.

This is the land where Robert Frost lived, and much of his poetry was inspired by scenes such as these. Tom and I hope that these correlations, the blending of the arts of poetry and photography, will bring pleasure to all who love the poetry of Robert Frost.

Betsy Melvin

FOREWORD

Theodore Morrison, whose friendship with Robert Frost started earlier than my own, has made the point that Frost is not a nature poet, in the Wordsworthian sense of the term, "but rather a poet who is also a countryman, who knows his birds and botany, his woods and farms and all their uses, too well to be fooled." I think Frost would have felt that many of the Melvins' pictures take the same knowing look: they see New England as the habitation of particular flora and fauna, with a predominant interest in the fauna called New Englanders, and their spoor.

Looking at the handsome account of Frost's country in these pages, one is struck by how completely the visual and the verbal experiences differ. The moment of revelation which the poet attends on is different from the photographer's, and the means by which he fixes it are different. Some effects, some visual images, may allow for literal translation of feeling, but most comparisons between pictures and poems can only hope to establish some sort of equivalence. I can't speak with a craftsman's authority about these photographs, and they don't need that. But some of Frost's verbal effects dramatize the difference between the two arts.

In "Hyla Brook," for instance, he speaks of the spring peepers, "That shouted in the mist a month ago/ Like ghost of sleigh-bells in a ghost of snow." That is perhaps as much physical experience as can be compressed into twenty syllables, yet it works directly neither on our visual nor our auditory imagination, but rather exists as an astonishing verbal experience. The playfulness of the image of ghosts is word-playfulness, which we translate only later into the aural and visual experiences. Peepers *do* sound like sleigh-bells (not everybody remembers the high, shrill dissonance of sleigh-bells), and early spring mist *can* impersonate the other vague white element it has lately supplanted. Our senses work like that, when surprised. But it is the sheer compression of those eighteen words, their focusing of the lens of simile, that makes the poem lodge itself in our verbal imagination. "The utmost of ambition is to lodge a few poems where they will be hard to get rid of," he wrote. "Hyla Brook" ends with the line, "We love the things we love for what they are." What poems *are*, of course, is an astonishment of words.

Frost's famous puns could be likened to the photographer's technique of double exposure. (Both devices require some sophistication, to make an insight out of a confusion). In "The Ax-Helve," when the French-Canadian craftsman has finished carving the helve and mounted the axhead, "he brushed the shavings from his knee/ And stood the ax there on its horse's hoof,/ Erect, but not without its waves, as when/ The snake stood up for evil in the Garden—"

Here the exposure (in the photographer's sense) is triple: there's the double meaning of *stood up for*, but there is also the echo of Milton's Latinism in *not without* and *as when*, which makes of the lines a playful incursion into what remains, for most of us, Milton's park. It is a scene Frost will pun on again in later years in a poem called "Away!", the only poem that treats directly on his own death:

> Don't think I leave
> For the outer dark
> Like Adam and Eve
> Put out of the Park.
>
> Forget the myth.
> There is no one I
> Am put out with
> Or put out by.

Then there is the texture of light you hear photographers talk about, which I believe has an equivalent in the poet's texture of sound. The poet sets his ear for a given scene the way a photographer sets his lens. Frost's poem " 'Out, out—' " tells of a boy whose hand is cut off by a saw-blade, and who dies as much from the realization as for any medical reason:

> The boy's first outcry was a rueful laugh,
> As he swung toward them holding up his hand
> Half in appeal, but half as if to keep
> The life from spilling. Then the boy saw all. . . .
>
> He saw all spoiled.

He saw all spoiled. The four words are *lighted* with a terrible light. Slow, accented syllables (*spondaic*, the prosodist calls them), they act out the grief with a bleak, drawn-out, voweled sound which it is not excessive to compare with Lear's heartbroken cry over the dead Cordelia, "Thou'lt come no more."

Frost had a wonderful ear for the way people declare themselves in speech—variously, and so as to identify both their character and some immediate dramatic response. He listened for these "sounds of sense" (as he called them) as much as to the data they overlay. He occasionally said, as his hearing dimmed in his later years, that he'd rather be blind than deaf. I think he meant by that only that his ears astonished him more than his eyes did. But his eyes were lesser only as a giant's toes may be shorter and less prehensile than his fingers. He looked with the same fierce attention that he listened with.

Once when I was driving him home from a visit to my college, I stopped for gas on the Connecticut Turnpike. Between the gasoline pumps hung large metal cylinders, perhaps three feet long and a foot in diameter, which I had not until then ever seen, though they'd been there since the turnpike opened. Frost asked me what they were. He kept hoping that my years as an aviator had made me attentive to mechanical things. But I had learned, the hard way, not to fake answers to him. So he asked the attendant, wiping his side of the windshield.

"They're for quick oil changes," the boy said. "You put one hose under the crankcase and the other in the top, and you can change oil as quick as you can fill a gas tank."

"Do you use them much?" Frost asked.

"Nope," the boy said.

"Why not?" He was interested.

"They don't work."

"Never did work?"

"Never did work."

Frost shared his pleasure at this successful exposure with me, but all the way to Cambridge I was looking at things with the attention of a madman, to see what else I hadn't seen. He was eighty-five, I was a dim-sighted forty, but in the kingdom of the dim-sighted, the man who pays attention is king.

I expect the Melvins would feel as diffident as I am (*scared* was the word I would have used when he walked the earth, though I loved him) to say what Frost would have made of these pictures; but I know he admired acts of attention.

William Meredith

Connecticut College
1976

So low for long they never right themselves:
You may see their trunks arching in the woods
Years afterward, trailing their leaves on the ground
Like girls on hands and knees that throw their hair
Before them over their heads to dry in the sun.
But I was going to say when truth broke in
With all her matter-of-fact about the ice-storm,
(Now am I free to be poetical?)
I should prefer to have had some boy bend them
As he went out and in to fetch the cows —
Some boy too far from town to learn baseball
Whose only play was what he found himself
                    Summer or winter and could play alone.
One by one he subdued his father's trees
By riding them down over and over again
Until he took the stiffness out of them
And not one but hung limp not one was left
For him to conquer. He learned all there was

Birches

When I see birches bend to left and right
Across the lines of straighter darker trees,
I like to think some boy's been swinging them.
But swinging doesn't bend them down to stay.
Ice storms do that. Often you must have seen them
Loaded with ice some sunny winter morning
After a rain. They click upon themselves
As the breeze rises, and turn many colored
As the stir cracks and crazes their enamel.
Soon the sun's warmth makes them shed crystal shells
Shattering and avalanching on the snow crust —
Such heaps of broken glass to sweep away
You'd think the inner dome of heaven had fallen.
They are dragged to the withered braken by the load
And they seem not to break; though once they are bowed

To learn about not launching out too soon
And so not carrying the tree away
Clear to the ground. He always kept his poise
To the top branches, climbing carefully
With the same pains you use to fill a cup
Up to the brim and even above the brim.
Then he flung outward feet first with a swish
Kicking his way down through the air to the ground.
So was I once myself a swinger of birches.
And so I dream of going back to be.
It's when I'm weary of considerations,
And life is too much like a pathless wood
Where your face burns and tickles with the cobwebs
Broken across it and one eye is weeping
From a twig's having lashed across it open.
I'd like to get away from earth a while
And then come back to it and begin over.

May no fate wilfully misunderstand me
And half grant what I wish and snatch me away
Not to return. Earth's the right place for love:
I don't know where it's likely to go better.
I'd like to go by climbing a birch tree
And climb black branches up a snow white trunk
Toward heaven, till the tree could bear no more,
But dipped its top and set me down again.
That would be good both going and coming back.
One could do worse than be a swinger of birches.

Robert Frost

See August Atlantic

BIRCHES

When I see birches bend to left and right
Across the lines of straighter darker trees,
I like to think some boy's been swinging them.
But swinging doesn't bend them down to stay.
Ice-storms do that. Often you must have seen them
Loaded with ice a sunny winter morning
After a rain. They click upon themselves
As the breeze rises and turn many-colored
As the stir cracks and crazes their enamel.
Soon the sun's warmth makes them shed crystal shells
Shattering and avalanching on the snow-crust—
Such heaps of broken glass to sweep away
You'd think the inner dome of heaven had fallen.
They are dragged to the withered bracken by the load,
And they seem not to break; though once they are bowed
So low for long, they never right themselves:
You may see their trunks arching in the woods
Years afterwards, trailing their leaves on the ground
Like girls on hands and knees that throw their hair
Before them over their heads to dry in the sun.
But I was going to say when Truth broke in
With all her matter-of-fact about the ice-storm
I should prefer to have some boy bend them
As he went out and in to fetch the cows—
Some boy too far from town to learn baseball,
Whose only play was what he found himself,
Summer or winter, and could play alone.

One by one he subdued his father's trees
By riding them down over and over again
Until he took the stiffness out of them,
And not one but hung limp, not one was left
For him to conquer. He learned all there was
To learn about not launching out too soon
And so not carrying the tree away
Clear to the ground. He always kept his poise
To the top branches, climbing carefully
With the same pains you use to fill a cup
Up to the brim, and even above the brim.
Then he flung outward, feet first, with a swish,
Kicking his way down through the air to the ground.
So was I once myself a swinger of birches.
And so I dream of going back to be.
It's when I'm weary of considerations,
And life is too much like a pathless wood
Where your face burns and tickles with the cobwebs
Broken across it, and one eye is weeping
From a twig's having lashed across it open.
I'd like to get away from earth awhile
And then come back to it and begin over.
May no fate willfully misunderstand me
And half grant what I wish and snatch me away
Not to return. Earth's the right place for love:
I don't know where it's likely to go better.
I'd like to go by climbing a birch tree,
And climb black branches up a snow-white trunk
Toward heaven, till the tree could bear no more,
But dipped its top and set me down again.
That would be good both going and coming back.
One could do worse than be a swinger of birches.

ROBERT FROST COUNTRY

Breathes there a bard who isn't moved
When he finds his verse is understood
And not entirely disapproved
By his country and his neighborhood?

On Being Chosen Poet of Vermont

O hushed October morning mild,
Thy leaves have ripened to the fall . . .

October

Tomorrow's wind, if it be wild,
Should waste them all. . . .

October

O hushed October morning mild,
Begin the hours of this day slow.
Make the day seem to us less brief. . . .

October

Retard the sun with gentle mist;
Enchant the land with amethyst. . . .

October

There where it is we do not need the wall . . .

"Before I built a wall I'd ask to know
  What I was walling in or walling out . . ."

Mending Wall

Good fences make good neighbors."

Mending Wall

And there might be a house we could buy
For only a dollar down . . .

A Serious Step Lightly Taken

O'er ruined fences the grape-vines shield
The woods come back to the mowing field . . .

Ghost House

I wondered who it was the man thought ground—
The one who held the wheel back or the one
Who gave his life to keep it going round . . .

(It ran as if it wasn't greased but glued) . . .

The Grindstone

I wondered what machine of ages gone
This represented an improvement on. . . .

The Grindstone

. . . The view was all in lines
Straight up and down of tall slim trees
Too much alike to mark or name a place by
So as to say for certain I was here
Or somewhere else: I was just far from home. . . .

The Wood-Pile

t was a cord of maple, cut and split
And piled—and measured, four by four by eight. . . .

The Wood-Pile

sions of half the world burned black
d the sun shrunken yellow in smoke. . . .

The Gum-Gatherer

Not yesterday I learned to know
The love of bare November days. . .

My November Guest

My Sorrow, when she's here with me,
Thinks these dark days of autumn rain
Are beautiful as days can be . . .

My November Guest

She loves the bare, the withered tree . . .
The faded earth, the heavy sky,
The beauties she so truly sees . . .

My November Guest

Autumn, yes, winter was in the wind . . .

Love and a Question

Whose woods these are I think I know. . . .

He will not see me stopping here
To watch his woods fill up with snow. . . .

Stopping by Woods on a Snowy Evening

But I have promises to keep,
And miles to go before I sleep . . .

Stopping by Woods on a Snowy Evening

The west was getting out of gold,
The breath of air had died of cold . . .

Looking for a Sunset Bird in Winter

"Our snow-storms as a rule
   Aren't looked on as man-killers, and although
   I'd rather be the beast that sleeps the sleep
   Under it all, his door sealed up and lost,
   Than the man fighting it to keep above it,
   Yet think of the small birds at roost and not
   In nests. Shall I be counted less than they are?" . . .

Snow

And yet to-morrow
They will come budding boughs from tree to tree . . .

Sno

Where a white birch he knew of stood alone . . .

Wild Grapes

Surely you wouldn't grudge the poor old man
Some humble way to save his self-respect. . . .

The Death of the Hired Man

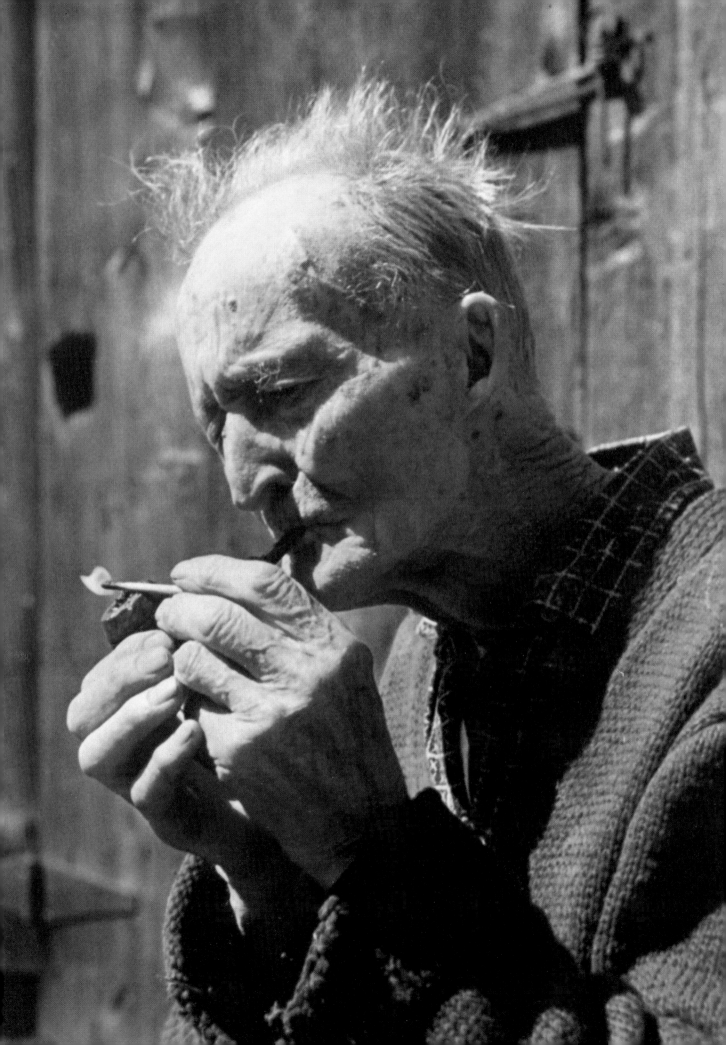

"I'll sit and see if that small sailing cloud
Will hit or miss the moon. . . ."

The Death of the Hired Man

How drifts are piled,
Dooryard and road ungraded,
Till even the comforting barn grows far away,
And my heart owns a doubt
Whether 'tis in us to arise with day . . .

Storm Fear

At four o'clock I shoulder axe
And in the afterglow
  link a line of shadowy tracks
Across the tinted snow. . . .

In Winter in the Woods Alone

Winter was only playing possum . . .
Two Tramps in Mud Time

"Speaking of contraries, see how the brook
In that white wave runs counter to itself. . . ."

West-running Brook

"It flows between us, over us, and *with* us.
And it is time, strength, tone, light, life and love . . ."

West-running Brook

Come, be my love in the wet woods, come,
Where the boughs rain when it blows. . . .

A Line-Storm Song

I have been one acquainted with the night.
I have walked out in rain—and back in rain.
I have outwalked the furthest city light. . . .

Acquainted with the Night

Oh, give us pleasure in the flowers today . . .

A Prayer in Spring

Keep us here
All simply in the springing of the year.
Oh, give us pleasure in the orchard white . . .

A Prayer in Spring

But he turned first, and led my eye to look
At a tall tuft of flowers beside a brook,
A leaping tongue of bloom the scythe had spared
Beside a reedy brook the scythe had bared. . . .

The Tuft of Flowers _

The butterfly and I had lit upon,
Nevertheless, a message from the dawn,
That made me hear the wakening birds around . . .

The Tuft of Flowers

ut still unstoried, artless, unenhanced,
ich as she was, such as she would become.

The Gift Outright

She is as in a field a silken tent . . .
Seems to owe naught to any single cord,
But strictly held by none, is loosely bound
By countless ties of love and thought
To everything on earth the compass round . . .

The Silken Tent

If tired of trees I seek again mankind,
Well I know where to hie me—in the dawn,
To a slope where the cattle keep the lawn. . . .

Vantage Point

As I came to the edge of the woods,
Thrush music—hark!
Now if it was dusk outside,
Inside it was dark. . . .

Come In

The last of the light of the sun
That had died in the west
Still lived for one song more
In the thrush's breast. . . .

Come In

"Where is your village? Very far from here?"
"There is no village—only scattered farms.
We were but sixty voters last election. . . ."

The Mountain

The mountain stood there to be pointed at
Pasture ran up the side a little way,
And then there was a wall of trees with trunks;
After that only tops of trees, and cliffs . . .

The Mountain

"There's a brook that starts up on it somewhere . . ."

The Mountain

"You and I know enough to know it's warm
Compared with cold, and cold compared with warm. . . ."

The Mountain

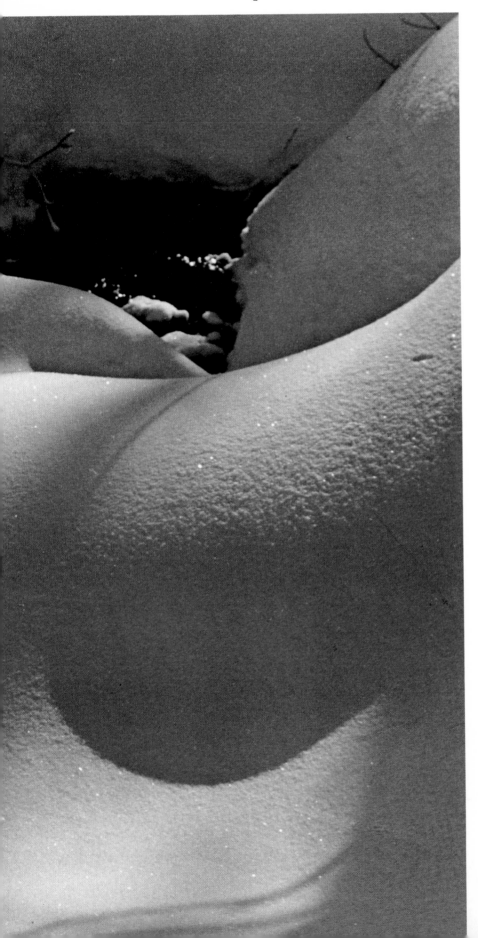

Often you must have seen them
Loaded with ice a sunny morning . . .
They are dragged to the withered bracken by the load . . .
You may see their trunks arching in the woods . . .

Birches

Life is too much like a pathless wood . . .

Birches

'd like to go by climbing a birch tree,
And climb black branches up a snow-white trunk
Toward heaven, till the tree could bear no more,
But dipped its top and set me down again.
That would be both good going and coming back.
One could do worse than be a swinger of birches.

Birches

Two roads diverged in a yellow wood,
And sorry I could not travel both
And be one traveler, long I stood . . .

The Road Not Taken

I took the one less traveled by,
And that has made all the difference.

The Road Not Taken

ILLUSTRATIONS

"Robert Frost" by KARSH OF OTTAWA

Photographs by BETSY AND TOM MELVIN:

"Sweet Harvest"
"Double Beauty"
"Vermont Countryside"
"Quiet Interlude"
"Blush of Autumn"
"Usefulness Outlived"
"Peaceful Border"
"Deserted"
"Sugar House Palette"
"Bygone Days"
"Rochester Range"
"Golden Forest"
"Sugaring Time"
"Götterdämmerung"
"Champlain's November Mood"
"Forest Murmurs"
"A Poem"
"Storm"
"Sudden Storm"
"Hallowed Hall"
"Champlain Gold"
"Winter Feathers"
"Common Aim"
"Lone Birch"

"The Old Wood-Carver"
"Moonlight in Vermont"
"Country Storm"
"Evening Star"
"Spring Snow"
"Tranquil Waterway"
"Bolton Brook"
"Trees in the Rain"
"Mount Mansfield, from Jericho"
"Sweet Pea"
"Spring's Symphony"
"Skyscrapers"
"Boat at Dawn"
"Youthful Forest"
"The Silken Tent"
"Randolph Dawn"
"Twinkling Forest"
"Autumn Nocturne"
"Woodstock Farm"
"Mansfield at Eventide"
"Riverlet"
"Rhythm"
"Frosty Bows"
"Dimension"
"Birches"
"The Road Not Taken"
"Cabin in the Clearing"

Betsy Blake Melvin was born in Springfield, Massachusetts. She graduated from Vermont Junior College and Principia College. A snapshooter from age eleven on, she entered into photography seriously in 1965. She studied with John Doscher, Adolph Fassbender, and at the New England Institute of Professional Photography; has had numerous one-woman shows around New England, including the Vermont State House, the University of Vermont, and at Saint Michael's, Trinity, Vermont and Middlebury Colleges. Mrs. Melvin has had several prints hung in the national competition of the Professional Photographers of America, and received dozens of state and regional awards for excellence.

Tom Melvin, born in Vienna, studied photography in Vienna, Lisbon, and New York; served professionally with the U.S. forces in China-Burma-India theater, and operated his own studio for twenty-six years in Philadelphia. In addition, he has instructed advanced portraiture in accredited schools and privately. He, too, has received numerous state and regional awards for his work.

"The Artistic Alliance" was formed when Betsy and Tom were married in 1971. They maintain two galleries of their work, in Burlington and Essex Center, Vermont.